Original publication: "Hudební nástroje. Klíček pro malé muzikanty 2."
Author: Eva Šašinková, M.M., Ph.D., M.B.A.
Illustrations: Mgr. Kateřina Kovářová
Original graphic design: Lumír Kaděra
Original publisher: Czech Music Edition, Prague, Czech Republic, 2022
Website: www.hudebni-publikace.cz
Copyright: Eva Šašinková, M.M., Ph.D., M.B.A.
Original Czech version ISBN: 978-80-908169-2-3

English adaptation: "Clefi's Musical Instruments"
Illustrations: Mgr. Kateřina Kovářová
Translation, adaptation, and graphic design: Roman Placzek, D.M.A.
Publisher: BumbleBeeNotes™ Music Publishing, Manlius, NY, USA, 2024.
Catalog number: cbbn002-wb-002
Website: www.bumblebeenotes.com
Copyright: BumbleBee Notes™ Inc. Music Corporation
ISBN: 979-8-9919035-1-6

Clefi's Musical Instruments

Eva Šašinková, M.M., Ph.D., MBA, the author of the series, lives in Prague, Czech Republic, where she concertizes and holds academic positions at the Pilsen Conservatory and Academy of Music in Prague. Since childhood, Eva has dreamed of becoming a music teacher, sharing her passion and experience of love for music, especially with children. She has a deep love for the double bass, her instrument, in which she holds a master's degree. However, Eva also profoundly admires the piano, an instrument that was an inseparable part of her childhood. This admiration is the reason behind the concept of her method, which she based on the keyboard's layout. Eva is convinced that the piano is a unique instrument designed to help explain the fundamentals of music theory, the meaning of tones and melody, and the mission of music. She successfully proves her firm conviction in the practical application of her method. The story of her project started with a children's story that came to life during a trying period in the author's life.

Her passion for teaching children and desire to share her knowledge helped her concentrate on the essentials. During her pedagogical activities, Eva noticed that the materials available to her for the curriculum presentation were not, in her professional opinion, satisfactory. She started to visit music schools in her home country, the Czech Republic, comparing, editing, reworking, and creating. As a result, Eva began to bring worksheets filled with information and fun activities to the music education classes to make students' time learning music theory more engaging, easily accessible, and entertaining. The reactions of the young music students and fellow pedagogues were overwhelmingly positive.

Professor Eva managed to engage children's senses from all angles—drawing, singing, and practical demonstrations on a keyboard—everything children appreciated. On top of that, she had "The Story of a Song, "which kicked off a star career for one little boy, Clefi. He welcomes children in his "Clefi's Little Notebook" and helps them learn more in the four volumes of his "Clefi's Music Notebook." He plays and sings with them in "Clefi's Little Music Education Notebook" (in the translated version integrated into "Clefi's Little Notebook" – editor's note) and "Clefi's Musical Instruments" written for little musicians. Clefi helps them practice their newly acquired knowledge in three workbooks full of fun tasks and exercises. Children play with little Clefi, learn, and get ready for the more dedicated encounter with Lady Music and their chosen instrument in a fun and engaging way. And maybe it will become the love of their lives, their calling, and a hobby, as it happened to the author.

And to the sad faces of those who did not have the luck to learn from the best teachers and publications and did not have the best opportunities, Eva says with her clever little smile: "If you love music and have an open heart, the muse will not ask you how old you are. She will kiss you on the brow when you least expect it. So do not wait and be ready!"

Author's Foreword

Clefi's New Music Education School
is a unified music education method for children, amateur musicians, and music students.

Based on my extensive multi-genre musical performing career, many years of experience teaching children, and my terminal education degree in music theory, I have created a unified music education program for children from an early age to young musicians who choose to study music more seriously. The New Music Education School leans on children's natural perception of music. It offers young musicians and their teachers a unified educational system of fundamental music theory aiming to support musical creativity. Its main goal is to awaken children's musicianship based on creativity and the ability to sing a song, play it on a musical instrument of their choice, and write it down correctly, the sort of musicianship that enables them to use their musical knowledge theoretically and practically.

The first book, Clefi's Little Notebook, is tailored for the youngest musicians. It introduces us to Clefi, a charming little boy who shares his story. Clefi becomes our companion on this musical adventure. In Clefi's Little Notebook, children delve into musical notation, the birth of a song, a musical note, a musical staff, a clef (which inspired Clefi's name), the musical alphabet, and a scale. They learn to read and write notes in the fourth, the middle octave, and practice their new skills through exercises, puzzles, engaging tasks, and songs they play and sing.

Clefi's Music Notebooks 1, 2, 3, and **4** follow Clefi's Little Notebook. These four full-color music textbooks stand out for their unique conceptual design. Each volume is a complete unit and can be used individually.

At the same time, all four volumes are designed as one method, seamlessly following one another, so that the children can acquire a complete knowledge of the fundamentals of music theory in a friendly and engaging way.

Beautiful illustrations and graphic design enhance the unique quality of these lovely publications. All textbooks are suitable for children, amateur musicians, and professional music students.

This music education series explains the fundamentals of music theory quickly and efficiently so that children can understand and practice them while playing musical instruments, singing, and harmonizing. These textbooks aim to develop children's musical abilities, aural skills, tone pitch and length perception, and rhythmical and tonal melodic structure.

The idea behind this methodological concept is to make children first listen, then understand, learn, utilize, and create. When born, a baby listens and absorbs speech. When it understands it, it tries to pronounce the first words. A child attempts to understand the connections and context. Only after several years can a child logically think and systematically create. And the same applies to the understanding of music! What would the knowledge of music theory be for if we did not listen to music and didn't use the ingenious system of music theory in practice? However, the same applies both ways. How can we expect to evolve in our music-making if we refuse to learn and explore the mysteries of music, its tonal relations, harmony, and rhythm?

This method will help children fully absorb the music and learn the essential human and life values through it. We can learn to read and write only if we can listen to our parents talk since early childhood. Then, we learn the words, pronounce them, and understand their meaning. The same applies to music and how we understand it.

I hope my books will bring you joy and help many young musicians open the door to the beautiful world of music.

Eva

What's Inside:

Hi, little future musicians,

And welcome back to my little music school! In this second book of my educational series, we will explore musical instruments. My story continues with the discovery of their origin. We will learn to recognize their characters and divide them into their appropriate families. I have prepared for you plenty of fun rhymes, a new story about how musical instruments came to be, picture coloring, and singing of new songs about musical instruments. I can't wait to start this journey with you. Together, we all will become little musicians in no time!

Yours, Clefi

MUSICAL SOUND

The **musical sounds** are made using **musical instruments**.

To make **rhythmical musical sounds**,
we use **rhythmic musical instruments**

 triangle

 drum

To make **melodic musical sounds**,
we use **melodic musical instruments**

The **melodic musical instruments** can play a song = **melody**.
A melodic sound is called a **TONE**.

trumpet

piano

violin

E Draw a musical instrument that makes **tones** = **melodic musical sounds**.

FIRST MUSICAL INSTRUMENTS

The historically first musical instruments were ordinary objects, such as **rattles, clay drums, wooden whistles,** and **animal horns.**

People made the first musical instruments
to accompany their singing or dancing.
The picture shows various instruments people used to make.

What objects did ancient people use to make musical instruments?

E Invent and draw your own prehistoric musical instrument. Then trace and color the picture of the prehistoric musician.

*How did the **first musical instruments** come to be?*
Perhaps the way it happened in the following story...

HOW LITTLE CLEFI BECAME A MUSICIAN

It's been a long time since little Clefi sang his first song. Since then, people have started singing about everything they see around them. Children loved to sing about animals, grownups about love, which made them happy, and young men's army service, which made everyone sad.

One Sunday afternoon, the neighbors got together as usual to talk and be merry. They had a reason since the harvest was excellent that year. Everyone brought something good to eat and drink, and some even brought little presents. Even the gamekeeper who lived in the house in the nearby forest came and brought an animal horn with him.

Very soon, they all started to sing. Clefi was there with his grandparents, listening to everyone, wishing he could do something to make it even more enjoyable. He noticed two pieces of wood by his feet and suddenly got an idea. He picked them up and started to hit one with the other into the song's rhythm. His grandpa, who was sitting next to him, watched him and began to smile, enjoying the way the sound of the wood enriched the song.

Clefi gave the sticks to Grandpa and picked up a clay bowl from the table. He put it on his lap and used his fingers to drum out the rhythm, this time like the rain hitting the roof. Everyone loved it and slowly started to join in.

One picked up a dry rattling plant, another two stones to add to the rhythm section, and the next person found a tin cup and a spoon. Their creativity grew as they all picked up something to play the music. It didn't take long, and someone finally got the idea to grab the animal horn and blow into it with all their might. The horn gave a deep, rich sound that made everyone stop in awe - but only for a little while. Soon, they were all singing and playing again with the curiosity that inspired the birth of new musical instruments.

And so, the first, most primitive musical instruments were born.

After that day, the only thing needed was for the neighbors to get together and try to bring something new and unique to make the others happy. And that's how people used everyday and newly invented objects to create rhythm. They also carved out the first whistles and flutes and built the first strumming musical instruments to create and accompany melodies.

E Color the picture with Clefi, his musical instruments, and his friend Birdy.

6

MODERN MUSICAL INSTRUMENTS

Today, we have many musical instruments. The instruments existing today are at the top of their evolution. They evolved gradually by perfecting the ancient musical instruments.

E Mark the prehistoric instruments and their modern versions.
- Circle the ancient musical instrument in **blue**,
- and the modern ones in **red**.

The person who makes the musical instruments is called the **instrument maker**. The instrument makers who make violins and other similar instruments are called **violin makers** or **luthiers**.

MUSICAL INSTRUMENTS FAMILIES

The musical instruments are divided into three main families:

THE PERCUSSIVE INSTRUMENTS - THE PERCUSSIONS

The musical instruments that we play by **striking**, **shaking**, or **scraping them**.

tambourine

drum

THE WIND INSTRUMENTS - THE WINDS

The musical instruments that we play by **blowing into them** with our mouths.

recorder

trumpet

THE STRING INSTRUMENTS - THE STRINGS

The musical instruments **with strings**. They are further divided according to the way we produce the sound on them:

We pluck and strum the STRUMMED ones -

guitar

We pluck and use bows with the BOWED ones -

violin

We press the keys to activate the hammers with the HAMMERED ones -

piano

"I Am a Musician"

is a beautiful Czech national folk song (on the next page).
It will accompany you throughout the book, and so Clefi wants to
ensure you understand and enjoy its lyrics. It's about musicians having
fun with instruments from all three instrumental families.

E Color as many rectangles as they are instruments in the picture.
Choose a different color for each instrumental group.

I Am a Musician

Clefi & Notelina's Songbook, pg. 20

2. I am a musician...
I play the violin. And how do you play it?
|:Fiddle, tweedle dee, and needle, fiddle, tweedle, violin!:| cotton bin.

3. I am a musician...
I will play my trumpet. And how do you play it?
|:Tantara-ra (3 times), my trumpet!:| your crumpet.

4. I am a musician...
I will play my guitar. And how do you play it?
|:Pluck and strum, pluck, (3 times), guitar pluck!:| ducks do quack.

5. I am a musician...
I play my piano. And how do you play it?
|:Cling and clang, and clang and cling, and cling and clang, piano cling!:| cling let it ring.

Learn and sing the song "I Am a Musician."

E Name the instruments in the picture and put them into the correct instrumental group.
- Color the percussive musical instrument **blue**,
- the wind instrument **yellow**,
- and the string instrument **brown**.

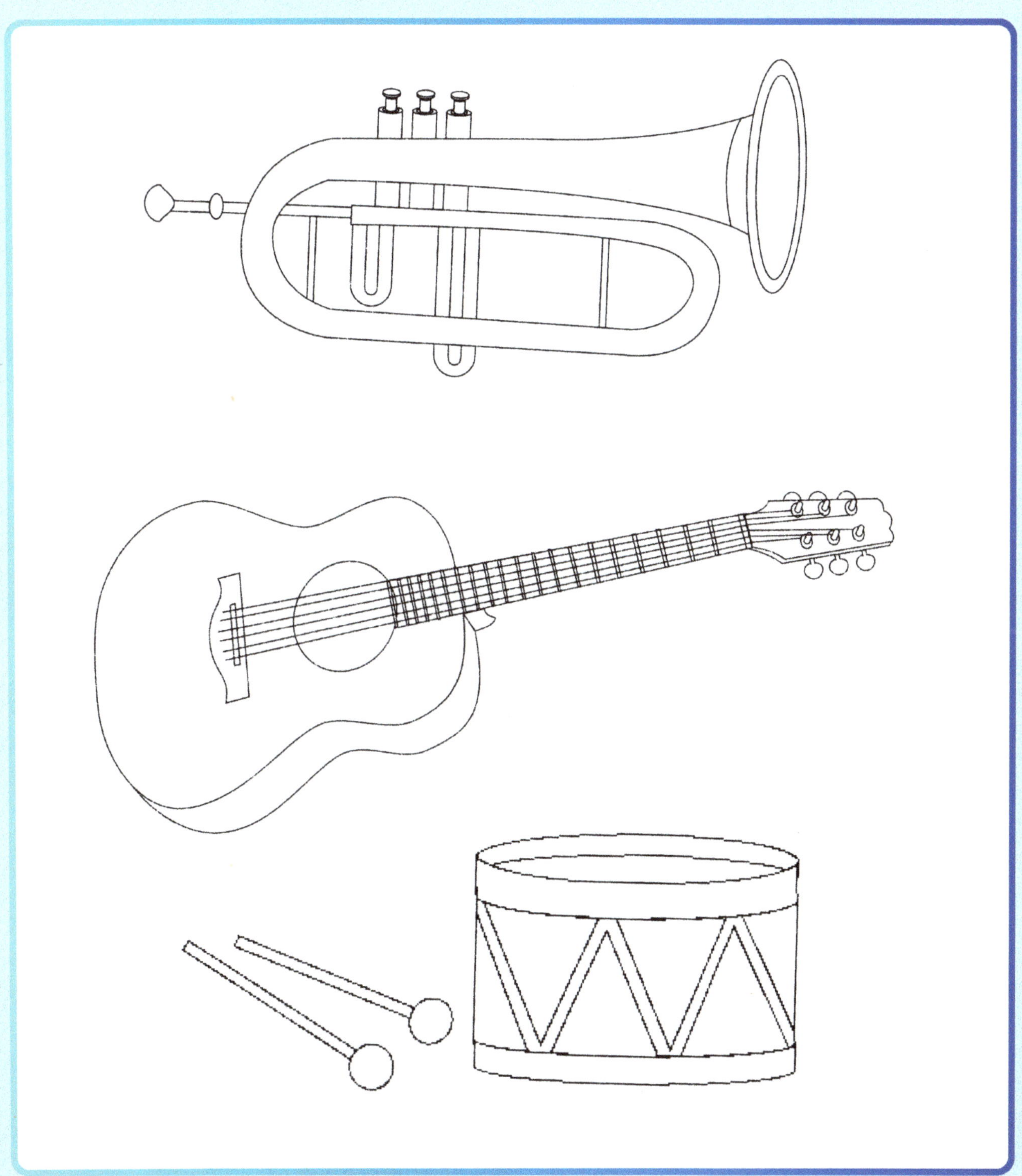

PERCUSSIONS

drum

I love to play my drum.
And how do you play it?
Boom taratat, boom taratat,
Boom taratat, little drum!

We play the percussive instruments, **the percussions,**
by **striking, shaking,** or **scraping** them.
They are the oldest musical instruments family.

tambourine

cymbals

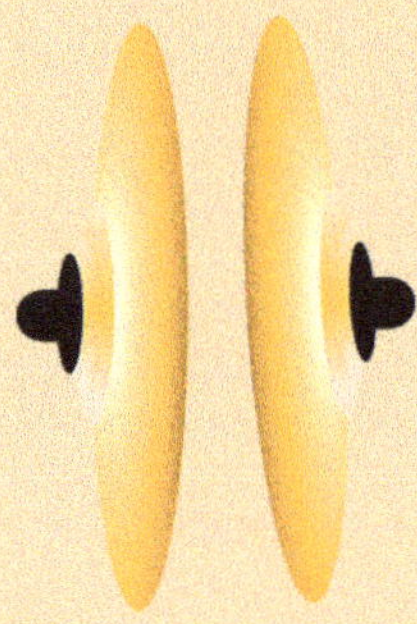

timpani
kettle drums

triangle

Drums and **timpani** are percussive instruments that produce sound by striking their **stretched membranes. Cymbals** and **triangles** are made of **metals.** They vibrate and resonate when struck.

Percussions I now know well
The triangle sounds like a bell
Cymbals give me a little scare
Timpani are hard to bear

E Connect the dots and color Clefi with his drum.

WINDS

I will play my trumpet.
And how do you play it?
Tantara-ra, tantara-ra,
Tantara-ra, my trumpet!

We play the **wind instruments** by **blowing into them** using our breath as the wind that makes them sound. The wind instruments can be **single-voice** or **multi-voice**.

The **single-voice wind instruments** produce only one voice. They are further divided into the **woodwinds** and the **brasses**.

To play **THE WOODWINDS**, we use either a **hole** to **blow into**, like when playing the flute, or the **reed**, **which vibrates** when the air **pushes on it**, like the clarinet, oboe, or bassoon.

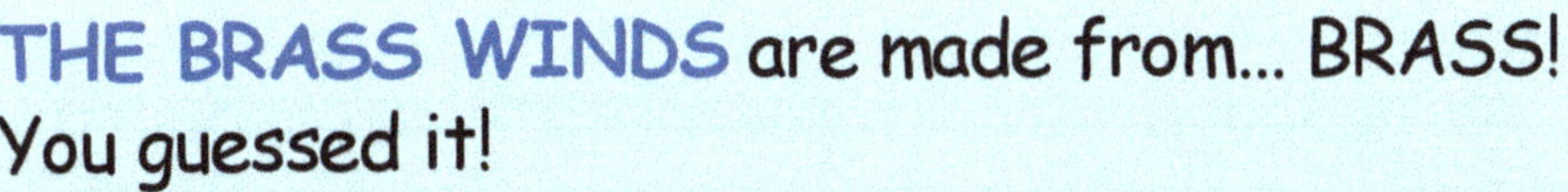

THE BRASS WINDS are made from... BRASS!
You guessed it!

We attach a **mouthpiece** to produce the sound
on **brass wind instruments** before blowing into
them.

Players manipulate the air pressure from their
breath with their lips in the mouthpiece to
create the desired sound.

E Carefully color the section with the assign colors. What instrument do you
see in the picture?

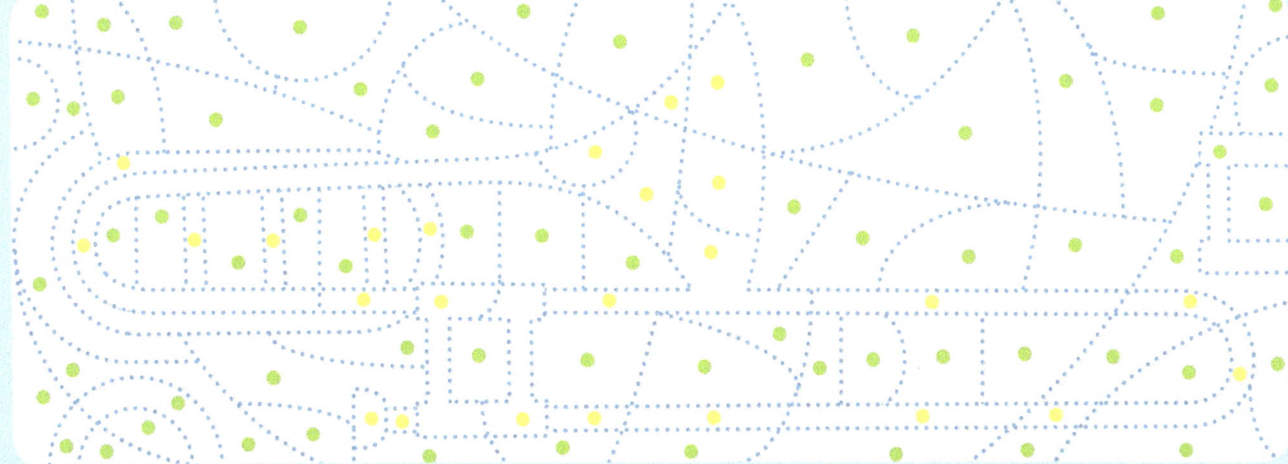

All wind instruments create sound through the **vibrations** produced by the **flowing air**. The wind instruments also include instruments that make sounds without the aid of a human breath, such as the **organ**.

The instruments capable of producing several voices simultaneously are called the MULTI-VOICE WIND INSTRUMENTS.

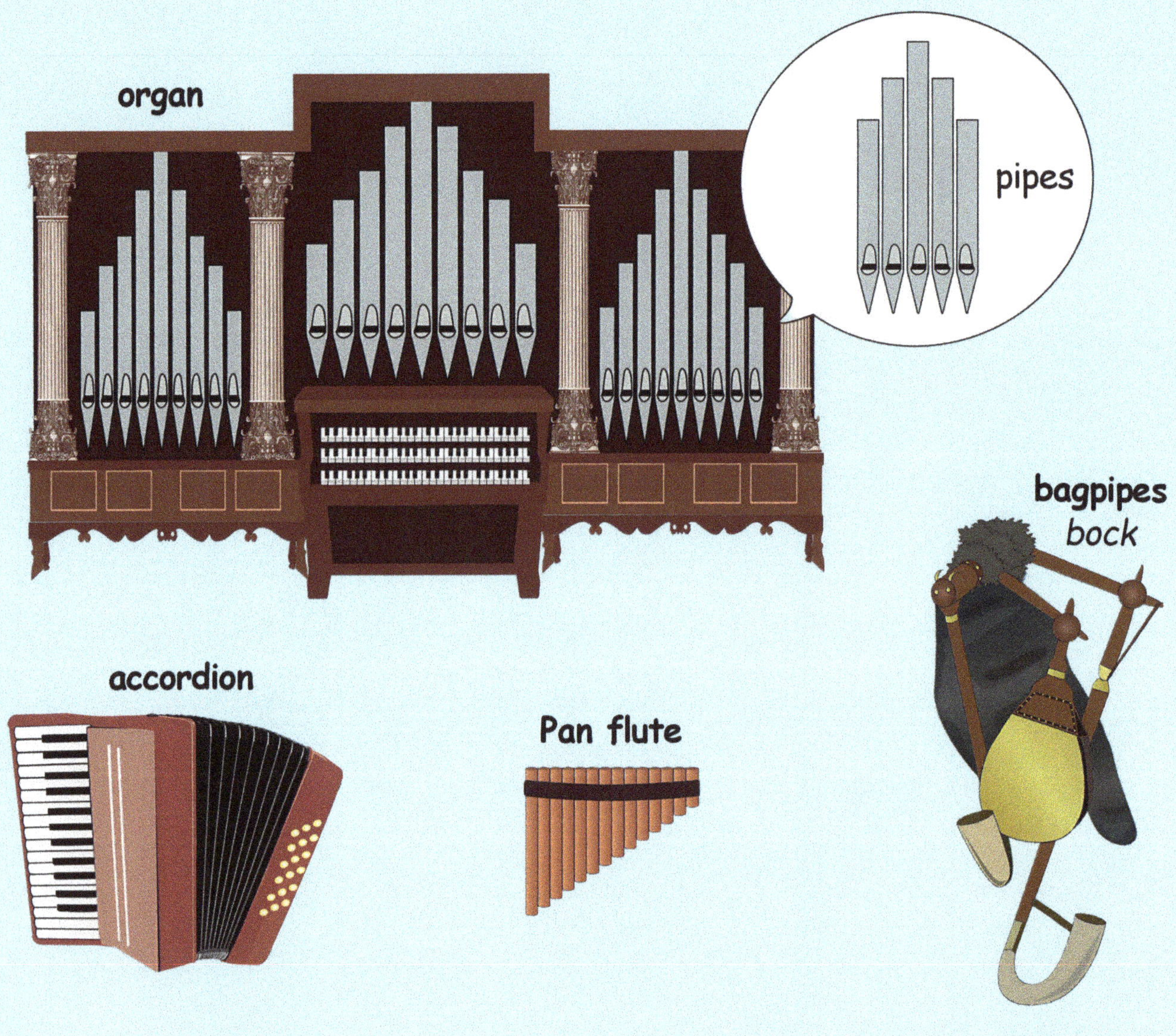

The **organ** has pipes. Air is forced into its pipes through a **sack**, which pressurizes it. Other wind instruments with a sack include the **accordion** and the **bagpipes** or the **bock**. The **Pan flute** and the **harmonica** are other examples of multi-voice wind instruments.

E ● Color the cart with the single-voice winds **green**,
● and the one with the multi-voice ones **yellow**.

Open your lungs
and take a deep breath
Get ready to pursuit

The trumpet is
the first step home
Then, tuba, clarinet, or flute

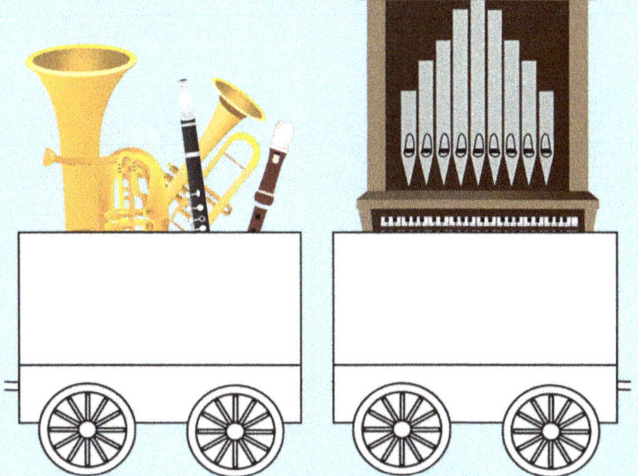

E Learn the poem. It will help you find the way home for Clefi who can step only on the squares with the **wind instruments**. Color them for him.

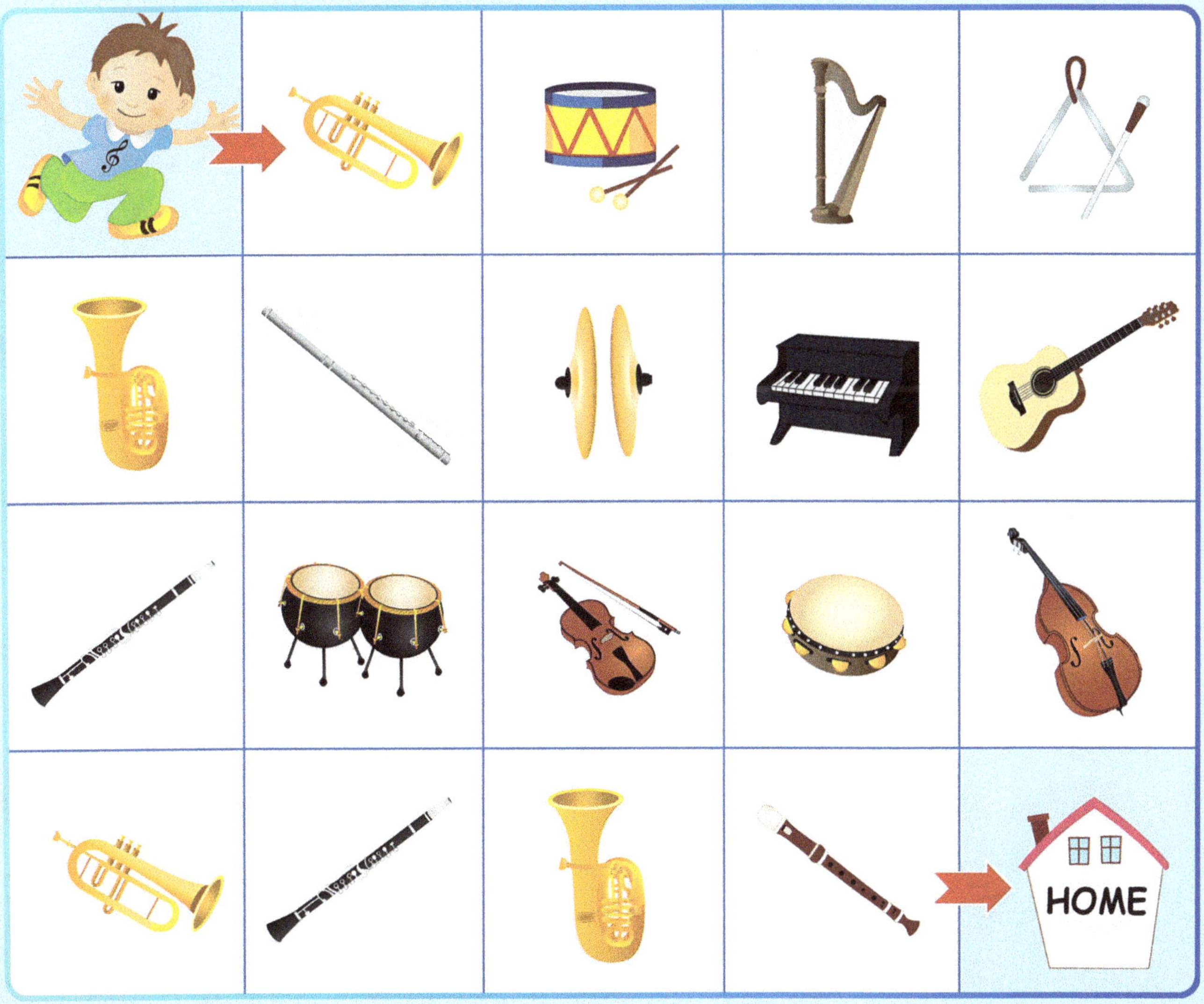

SONGS ABOUT PERCUSSIONS AND WINDS

Little Vixen Under a Tree
Clefi & Notelina's Songbook, pg. 26

Mean Bagpiper
Clefi & Notelina's Songbook, pg. 9

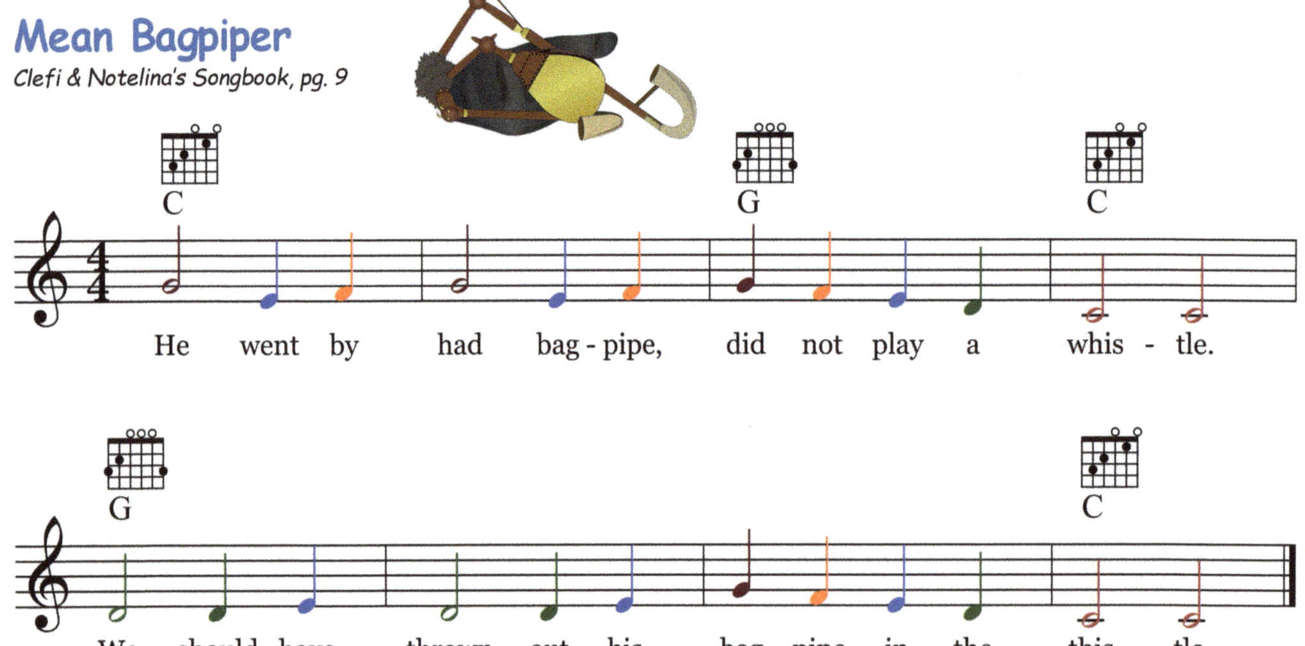

The Little Drummer
Clefi & Notelina's Songbook, pg. 22

C   F   G   C
The lit - tle drum - mer   drum - ming,   drum - ming on his   drum.

G   D   G
Cal - ling all his   friends to   go out and have   fun:

G7   C   G7   C
"Time to play and   have fun out-side.   Chase the squirl and   seek when we hide.

G   C   G7   C
Hol - a,   hol - a,   hey!   Let's en - joy this   day."

19

STRINGS

All **STRING INSTRUMENTS** have strings.
The difference is how we make them sound. We divide the instruments according to the way we play them into three families: **strummed**, **bowed**, and **hammered**.

We put all three families into their own houses.

Get to know the instruments
That sound thanks to their strings
Visit all their little houses
Where each of them now sings

The first house
is strumming with the plucky sound of
the guitar and its relatives.

The second house
is filled with the soothing sound
of the bowed instruments family.

The third house, the biggest one, is
filled with chatter of keys, hammers,
and strings living happily together under
one keyboard roof.

1. THE STRUMMED STRING INSTRUMENTS

are the instruments we play by plucking or strumming using the fingers.

2. THE BOWED STRING INSTRUMENTS

are the instruments we play using a bow. We can also pluck and strum them.

3. THE HAMMERED STRING INSTRUMENTS

produce sound by striking the strings with special hammers.
The keyed hammered string instruments, like the piano, have a **keyboard** that facilitates the movement of the hammers.
The hammered string instruments without a keyboard, like the cimbalom, are played using special hand-held hammers.

E Color as many apples as there are string instruments in the picture.

The string instrument family is the largest and most diverse instrumental family, but they all need strings to produce sound.

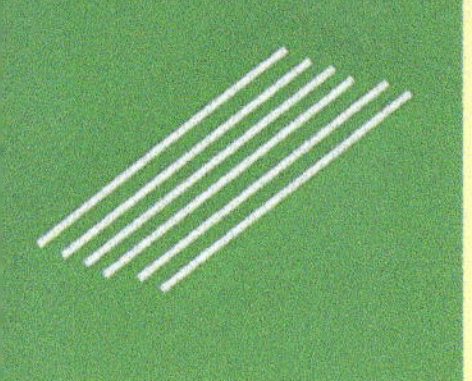

STRUMMED STRING INSTRUMENTS

I will play my guitar.
And how do you play it?
Pluck and strum, pluck,
Pluck and strum, pluck,
Pluck and strum, pluck, guitar pluck!

The **STRUMMED STRING INSTRUMENTS** have strings that we make vibrate by plucking or strumming them with our fingers.

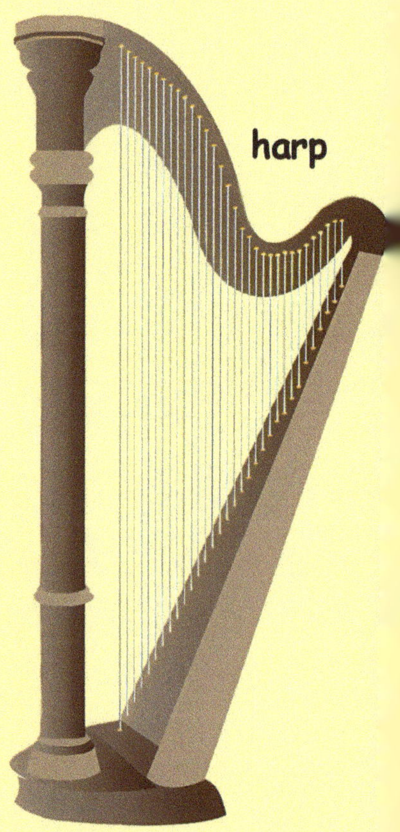

In movies about princesses, we often see the **lute**. The **lute** is the predecessor of today's **guitar**, which is the most popular strummed string instrument. One of the oldest, if not the oldest, is the **harp**, and the youngest is the **modern banjo**.

A long time ago, music became part of life in the castles. The children from the noble families were learning music and played musical instruments.

E Color the picture.

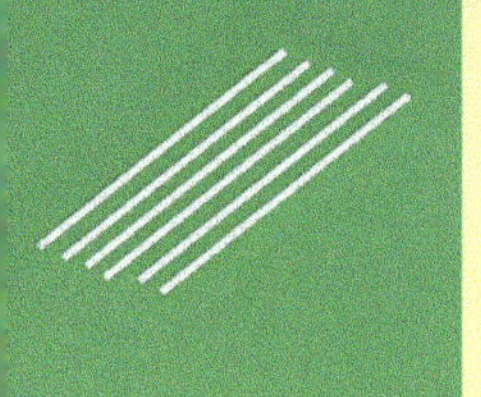

BOWED STRING INSTRUMENTS

I play the violin.
And how do you play it?
Fiddle, tweedle dee, and needle,
Fiddle, tweedle, violin!

The **BOWED STRING INSTRUMENTS** are played using a bow, which is a wooden stick with horsehair stretched from end to end.

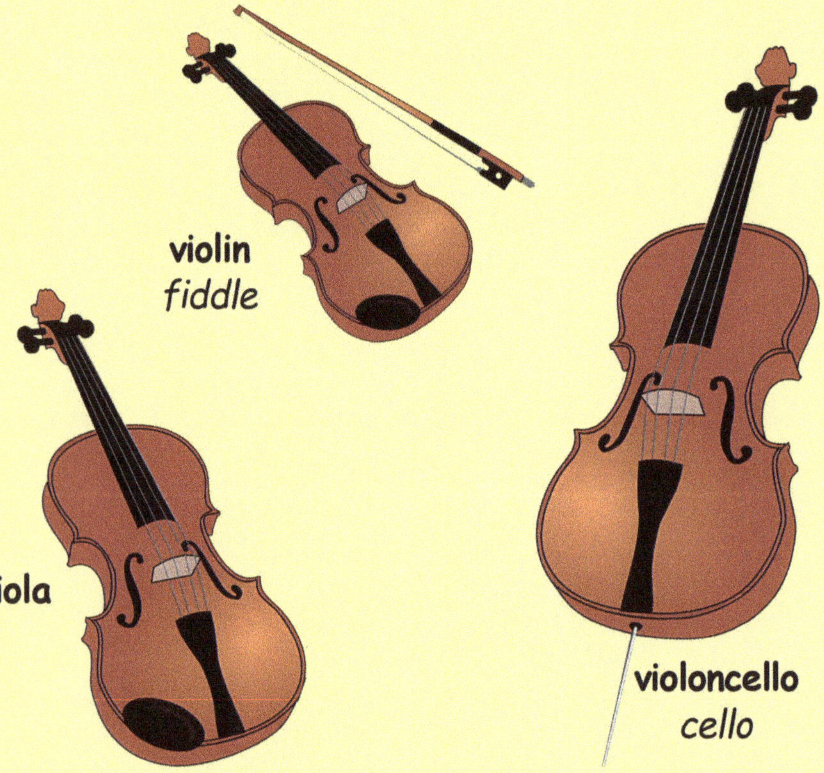

violin
fiddle

viola

violoncello
cello

double bass
bass

Today, we have four bowed string instruments. Their main differences are their size and the height of the tones they produce. We hold the **violin** and **viola** under the chin while the **violoncello** and the **double bass** have endpins for floor support.

The **violin** is the smallest bowed string instrument.
It plays the highest notes.

The **double bass** is the largest bowed string instrument.
It plays the lowest notes.

The **two fundamental clefs** are named
after these two instruments.

Treble or Violin Clef

is used for
high-pitched
voices and
instruments.

Bass Clef

is used for
low-pitched
voices and
instruments.

E ● Trace the treble - violin clefs in red,
● and the bass clefs in blue.

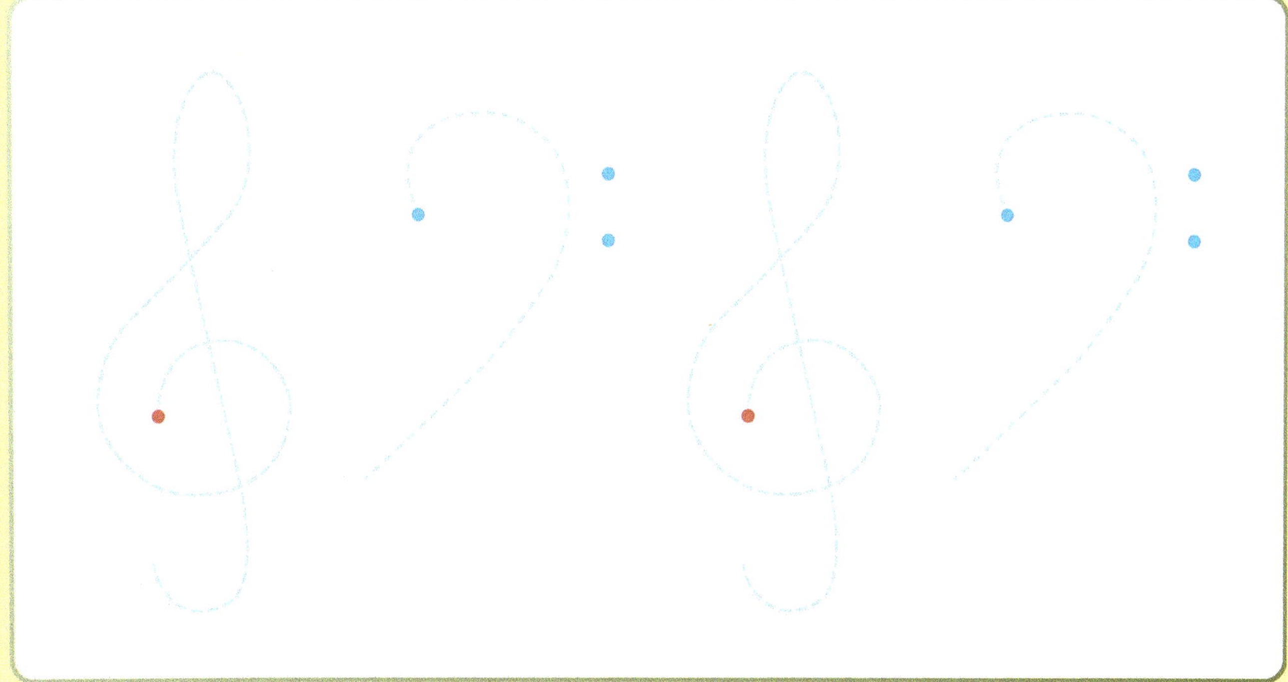

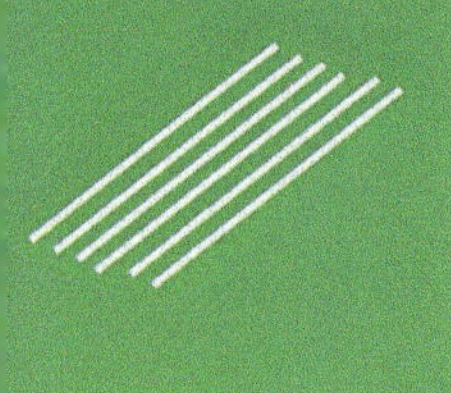

KEYBOARD
STRING INSTRUMENTS

I play my piano.
And how do you play it?
Cling and clang, and clang and cling,
And cling and clang, piano cling!

The **KEYED HAMMERED STRING INSTRUMENTS**, also known as **KEYBOARD INSTRUMENTS**, produce sound by using **keys** that, when pressed, **trigger hammers** to **strike** the **strings**.

piano
upright

piano
grand

The upright piano and concert grand piano are the primary examples of keyboard instruments. The concert grand piano has a distinctive wing-like shape and is referred to as **the wing** in some countries.

The **KEYBOARD** is made of **white** and **black keys.**
The **white keys** are larger. They are the **primary keys.**
All their tones belong to the **primary tone row.**

C D E F G A B

The **black keys** are smaller and raised above the white keys.

E Can you help Clefi to get to the piano?

E

Color the keys correctly, as they should be.

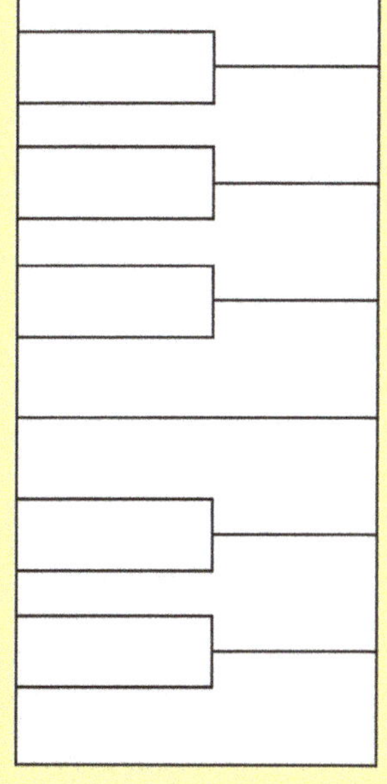

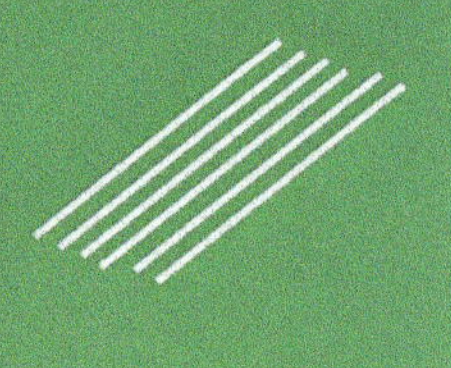

KEYBOARDLESS HAMMERED STRING INSTRUMENTS

The **cimbalom** is an excellent example of a hammered string instrument without a **keyboard**. The strings are played by striking them with specially designed **spoon-shaped hammer sticks with cotton-wrapped tips**.

Hey, Musicians, Whatcha Doin'?

Clefi & Notelina's Songbook, pg. 24

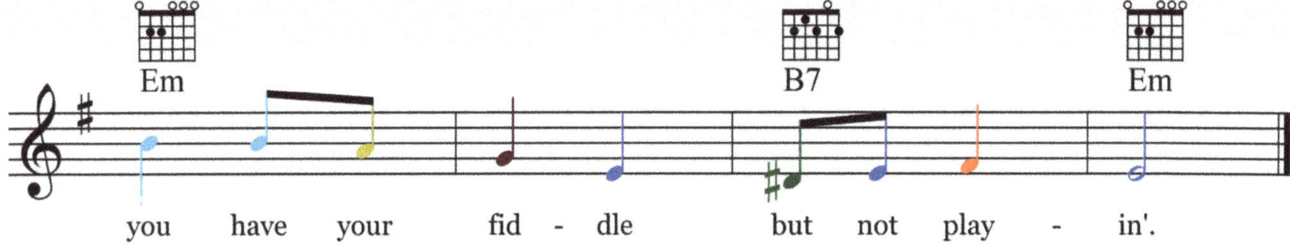

2. Play the fiddle, play the violin. Play the fiddle, play the violin.
   I wanna see those bridesmaids smilin', I wanna see those bridesmaids smilin'.

3. Play **cimbalom**, play it for me. Play cimbalom, play it for me.
   And make my love bride shine with glee, and make my love bride shine with glee.

4. Now, the bass, it's time for you, too. Now, the bass, it's time for you too.
   So there is no one sad in my crew, so there is no one sad in my crew.

5. All of you now play in one key. All of you now play in one key.
   And all together come home with me, and all together come home with me.

E Color the flowers as follows:
- ● the strummed instruments orange
- ● the bowed instruments green
- ● the hammered instruments blue

Flowers hide all that you know
Right colors now must do
Give everything its rightful name
Then color Clefi, too

When I Was a Little Boy
Clefi & Notelina's Songbook, pg. 27

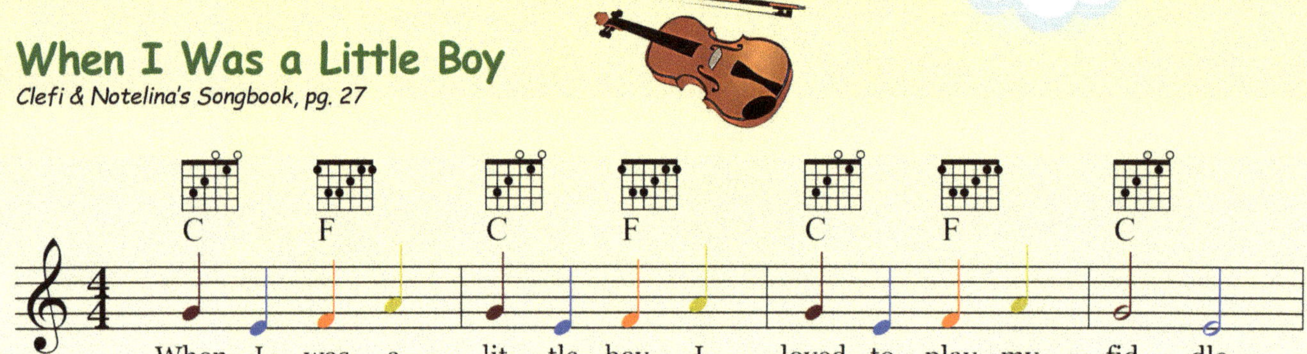

The Bass Behind Our Stove
Clefi & Notelina's Songbook, pg. 28

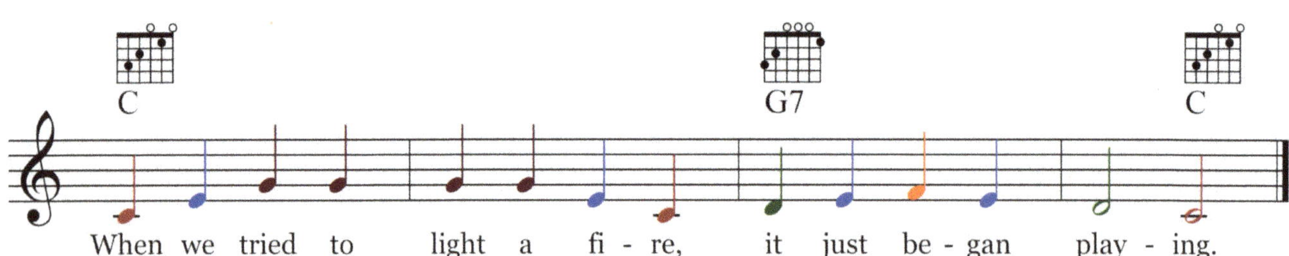

I Love Making My Harp Ring

Clefi & Notelina's Songbook, pg. 29

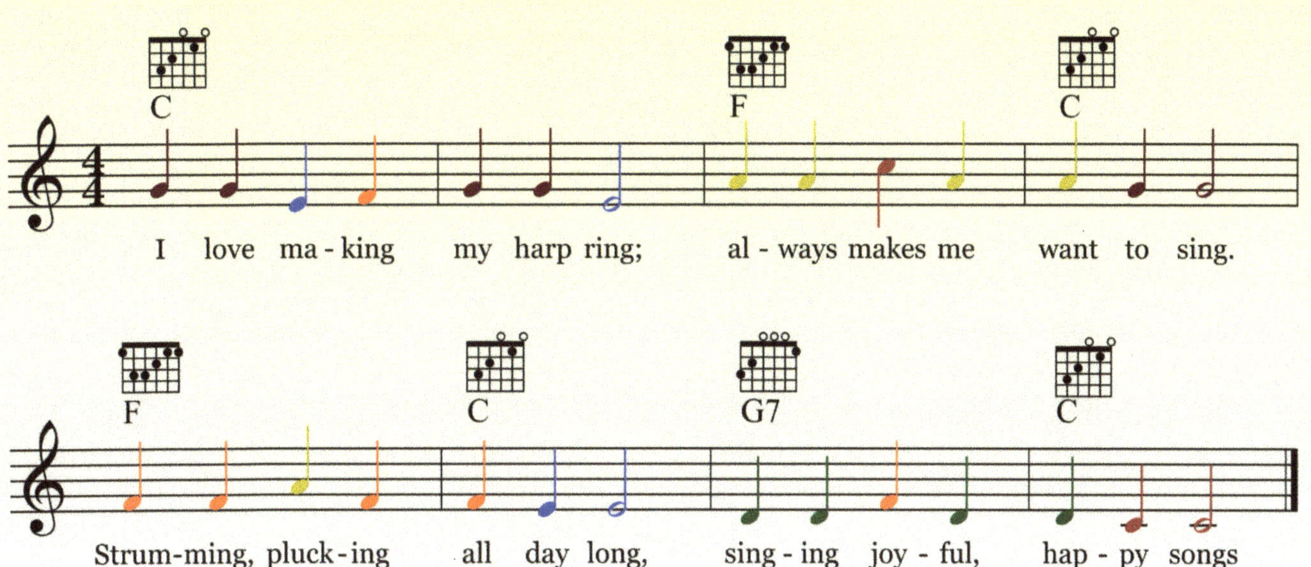

E Name all the instruments in the picture, then color it.

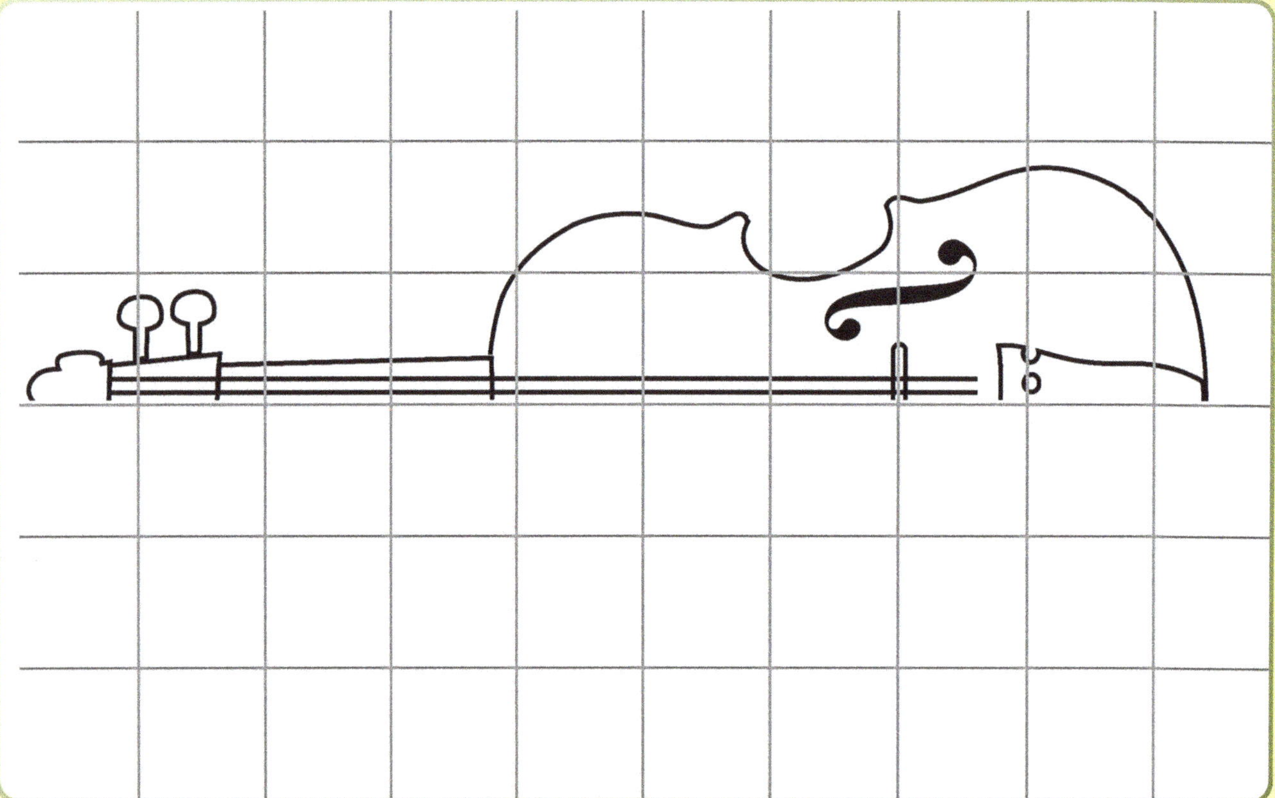

E Finish the drawing. What instrument do you see? What instrumental family does it belong to?

Clefi drew two identical pictures inspired by the songs, but there might be eight differences. Can you find them?

8 DIFFERENCES

CLEFI'S REVIEW

Now, you know many musical instruments. Just look around. Let's
see what you remember.

E Write the name of the instruments on this page into the
spaces next to them.

E Color the houses on the next page with their assigned colors:
- the woodwinds **brown**
- the brasses **yellow**
- the multi-voice wind instruments **red**
- the strings **blue**
- the strummed string instruments **pink**
- the hammered keyboard instruments **green**
- the percussions **orange**

A FEW ADDITIONAL FACTS

THE PERCUSSIONS

have been known since prehistoric times. In the beginning, these instruments were used mainly for the rhythmical accompaniment of dance and dancing rituals. Today, we have a large and diverse spectrum of percussive instruments. The instruments in this book represent the most common ones.

The drums and **the timpani** are **membranophone instruments**. We play them by **striking a stretched membrane** with **a hand** or **drumsticks**. Because of their shape, timpani are also known as kettle drums or kettles. They are mainly used in symphony orchestras.

The cymbals and **the triangle**, both **idiophone instruments**, produce their unique sounds by **striking** and **reverberating their metal**. The cymbals, two metal plates, are played by striking them against each other, while the triangle is played using a thin metal stick with a handle.

THE WIND INSTRUMENTS

The ancient wind instruments included various types of whistles made from bamboo and animal bones and horns. The wind instruments include all instruments that create the sound by **vibrating the air**. They can be by uni-voice or multi-voice.

THE UNI-VOICE WIND INSTRUMENTS

can play just **one voice**. They include the woodwinds and the brass instruments. The instruments in these two groups were made primarily of **wood** or **brass**, which gave them their group names. The main difference between the woodwinds and the brasses is how they create the sound.

The woodwinds

have **a hole** to use for blowing, like **the flutes** or **a reed** that vibrates when exposed to air pressure, such as **clarinet**, **oboe**, and **bassoon**. Because of this classification, we count **the traverse flute** (which was initially made of wood) and **the saxophone** among the woodwinds, even though they are made of metal.

The brass instruments or brasses

have mouthpieces that are used to blow into them. The mouthpieces are attached to the instruments, and the tone is created inside them by players manipulating their lips and the airflow. The brass instruments are usually made from thin brass, usually of polished yellow coloring. The brass players must maintain healthy teeth, flexible lips, and a quick tongue. Playing all wind instruments requires correct breathing technique and habits.

THE MULTI-VOICE WIND INSTRUMENTS

are capable of producing several voices simultaneously. They included instruments with and without a keyboard.

The organ, portatif (portative), and accordion have a keyboard and a sack to help pressurize the flowing air. These instruments are not played using the human breath. The portatif is a smaller instrument resembling the organ. It was used in smaller spaces and was "portable," hence the name. Some were so small that the player could carry it hang around their neck. Another instrument that uses a sack is the bagpipe and the bock (a type of bagpipes).

The multi-voice instruments include some that are played by blowing into, like the harmonica or Pan flute. The Pan flute is a primitive predecessor of the organ. It also has pipes, but not as many. The largest organ in the world is in Philadelphia. It has more than 28,000 pipes.

THE STRINGS

is the largest and most diverse instrumental group, with all instruments having strings.

THE STRUMMED STRING INSTRUMENTS

are played by strumming or plucking their strings with our fingers.

The guitar is the most widely used and popular strummed string instrument. It is used in a broad and diverse range of musical styles as a solo or accompanying instrument.

The harp is the strummed instrument with the highest string count. The modern harp, used in orchestras and as a solo instrument, has 47 strings. The harp is one of the oldest musical instruments in history. The oldest harps appeared more than 17,000 years ago. Small haps called lyres were invented by modifying the harp's shape from one bow to two upright arms connected by the crossbar. Both instruments are very old.

The banjo is a strummed string instrument that does not have a typical wood-made body but a circular drum with a stretched membrane that amplifies the sound. The banjo originated in West Africa and was introduced to Americans through the Caribbean slave trade. Today's banjo evolved in North America. It is popular in country music and many other popular musical genres.

The lute is the guitar's predecessor. It was a popular instrument with minstrels, troubadours, and trouveurs, the wandering singers, many of who were of noble descent.

THE BOWED STRING INSTRUMENTS

are played with the use of **the bow.** A bow is a wooden tension stick strung with quality horse-tail hair stretched from the tip of the bow to the frog. All modern string instruments are generally very similar, with the main differences being their size and the pitches they can produce.

The smallest bow string instrument, **the violin**, can play the highest pitches, and the largest one, **the double bass**, plays the lowest pitches. **The violin** and **viola** are held under the chin, supported by the left arm, while **the violoncello** **(cello)** and **the double bass** **(bass)** use the endpin to provide support for the players who sit or stand while playing them.

THE HAMMERED STRING INSTRUMENTS

These instruments produce sound by **special hammers striking the strings.**

The hammered string instruments WITH KEYBOARD

are also called simply **keyboard instruments** because they have several keys in one or more rows. These instruments make their strings vibrate by **the strike of the special hammers.** Every key has a little hammer that targets its specific string or a group of equally tuned strings. **The concert grand piano**, sometimes called "the wing" because of its shape, and the **upright piano**, invented for smaller spaces, are the best examples of this string family group.

The hammered string instruments WITHOUT KEYBOARD

are best represented by **the hammered dulcimer** and **the cimbalom.** We play these instruments by **striking the strings with special handheld hammers** made of wood and sometimes with cotton-wrapped tips. Both instruments are used in many diverse cultures, mainly in folk music.

Electric instruments, including keyboards, hybrid pianos, electric guitars, cellos, violins, and bass guitars, represent a hallmark of the modern era. They produce their unique sound by amplifying vibrations using electric current and sophisticated electronic components.

ONE LAST TEST

Connect the clouds that belong together.

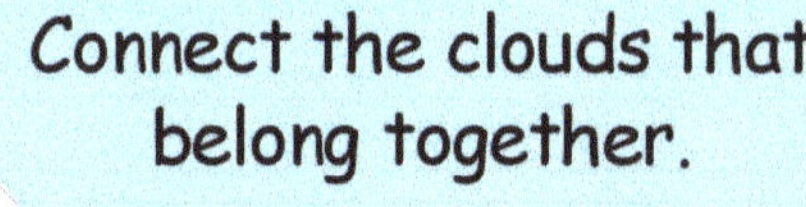
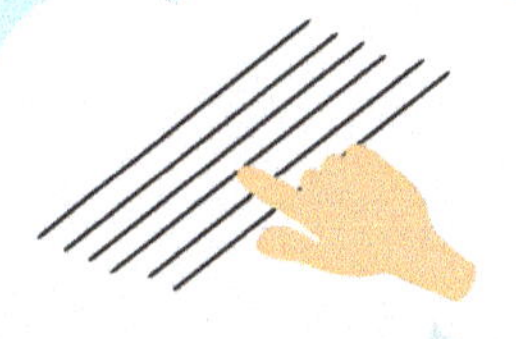

And now, you know all of these and many more musical instruments!

CERTIFICATE

OF COMPLETION

This certificate is presented to:

For successfully completing
Clefi's Musical Instruments

music education teacher

Clefi's Little American-British Music Dictionary

Music is a universal language; that is true. However, every nation uses its own beautiful tongue to describe and teach music. Clefi is originally Klíček, a little Czech boy who guides children through the fundamentals of music theory using the Czech language and music terminology. His American twin brother Clefi had to translate and adapt the text so English-speaking children could enjoy the journey. However, not all English-speaking musicians use the same music terms. Therefore, Clefi created this little American-British Music Dictionary of music terms used in Clefi's Little Notebook to accommodate our British-English-speaking music friends.

Note Values

Whole note	**Semibreve**
Half note	**Minim**
Quarter note	**Crotchet**
Eighth note	**Quaver**

Note Distances

Whole step	**Tone**
Half step	**Semitone**

Octaves

Fourth octave	**One-line octave**
Fifth octave	**Two-line octave**

Notes

C4-B4	**c'-b'** (one-line c-b)
C5	**c''** (two-line c)

Join Clefi's musical family!
Clefi invites you to visit his dedicated webpage and explore the enchanting musical world
of Dr. Eva's New Music Education School Series. Learn more about the author and about
the content of every volume of the series, dive into engaging materials, find answers to
all the exercises, discover more songs, and further deepen your love and understanding
of music and music education. Come make music with us!

www.bumblebeenotes.com/clefis-musical-world

www.bumblebeenotes.com/music-publishing